T0197391

To order additional copies of this book, contact:
Xlibris
844-714-8691
www.Xlibris.com
Orders@Xlibris.com

ISBN: 979-8-3694-1656-3 (sc)
ISBN: 979-8-3694-1657-0 (hc)
ISBN: 979-8-3694-1655-6 (e)
Library of Congress Control Number: 2024903634
Print information available on the last page

Rev. date: 02/14/2024

Once upon a time, there lived a mischievous little rabbit named Curious Charlie in the sunny town of Happyville.

Charlie had big floppy ears, a fluffy white tail, and a heart filled with boundless curiosity.

Always on the lookout for exciting adventures, he loved exploring every nook and cranny.

Chapter 1:

The Emotion in Happyville, everyone was usually happy, but sometimes, even Charlie got a little angry.

One day, he discovered a strange powerful feeling bubbling up inside him.

It was anger! Flames seemed to leap from his ears, and his fluffy tail stood on end.

Charlie realize that he needed to learn how to control his fiery emotion.

Chapter 2:

The wise Owl's Lesson Determined to understand his anger. Charlie sought guidance from Wise Old Owl, the town's resident sage.

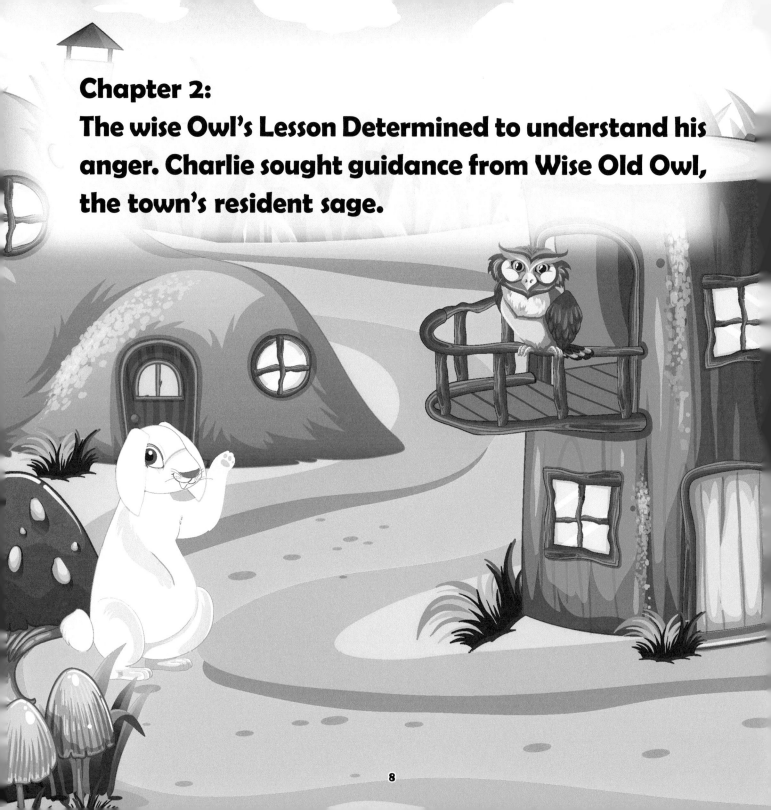

Owl explained that although anger was a natural emotion, it needed to be channeled positively.

He taught Charlie how to take deep breaths, count to ten, and find a peaceful place to cool down whenever anger threatened to overpower him.

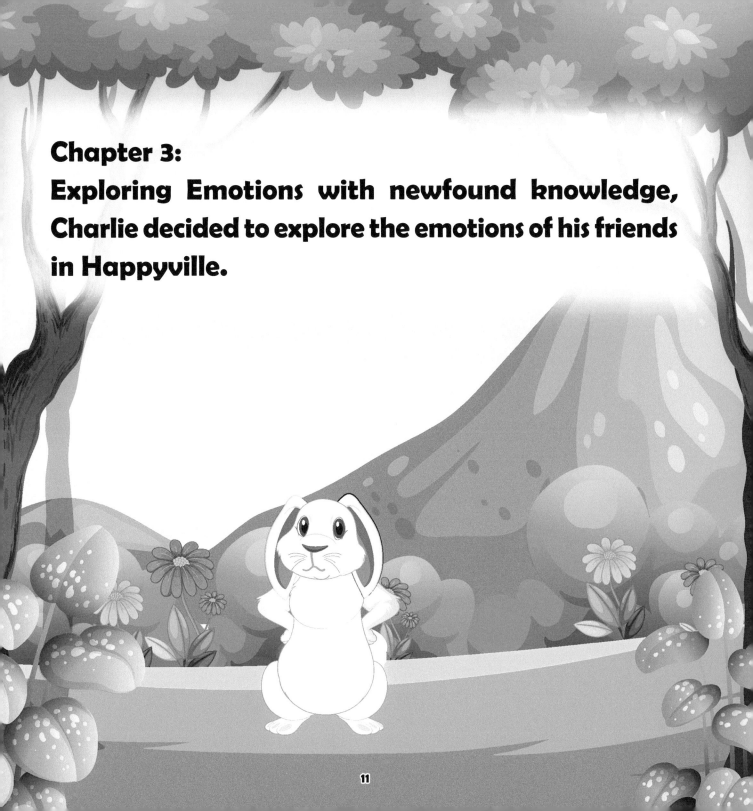

Chapter 3:
Exploring Emotions with newfound knowledge, Charlie decided to explore the emotions of his friends in Happyville.

He discovered that everyone from Excited Ellie the Elephant to Joyful Jimmy the Giraffe, experienced different feelings.

Charlie realized that anger was a part of life, but it didn't have to control him.

Chapter 4:
During the Silly Solution of his adventure, one day, Charlie discovered a special hidden spot in the middle of Happyville.

Guess what? He found a magical box filled with laughter and silliness! Whenever he felt angry, Charlie realized that laughing or making funny faces could make the anger disappear.

Laughter became his special superpower to fight against anger!

Chapter 5:

Sharing the wisdom and eagerness to help others, Charlie shared what he had learned about anger with his friends.

They formed a club called "The Emotion Explorers" and promised to support one another through all their ups and downs.

Together, they practiced deep breathing, counted to ten, and laughed away their anger, thus transforming Happyville into an even happier place.

Conclusion:

And so, Curious Charlie and his friends learned that anger was a normal part of life, but it could be tamed through understanding, practice, and laughter.

They understood that by talking about their feelings and finding happy ways to show them, they could change anger into something strong and fill their hearts with happiness.

Remember little ones, whenever you find yourself angry, just take deep breaths, count to ten, and embrace the power of laughter.

With curiosity and kindness, you can conquer any wild anger that comes your way.

The End.

Author's Note:

Remember, children, it's essential to talk to a trusted adult about your feelings and seek their guidance. They will always be there to help you understand and manage your emotions.

Printed in the United States
by Baker & Taylor Publisher Services